SEYMOUR CENTRE & THE
BIG ANXIETY – FESTIVAL OF
ARTS+SCIENCE+PEOPLE
PRESENT

GRACE UNDER PRESSURE

by David Williams & Paul Dwyer
in collaboration with the Sydney Arts & Health Collective

SEYMOUR | THE UNIVERSITY OF **SYDNEY**
GREAT IDEAS

THE BIG ANXIETY festival of arts + science + people

Currency Press,
Sydney

CURRENT THEATRE SERIES

First published in 2017
by Currency Press Pty Ltd,
PO Box 2287, Strawberry Hills, NSW, 2012, Australia
enquiries@currency.com.au
www.currency.com.au

Cataloguing-in-publication data for this title is available from the National
Library of Australia website: www.nla.gov.au

Typeset by Dean Nottle for Currency Press.
Cover design by Alphabet Studio.

Currency Press acknowledges the Traditional Owners of the Country on which
we live and work. We pay our respects to all Aboriginal and Torres Strait
Islander Elders, past and present.

Contents

Grace Under Pressure was first produced by Seymour Centre and the Big Anxiety (Festival of Arts + Science + People) at the Seymour Centre, Sydney, on 25 October 2017, with the following cast:

Performers	Renee Lim
	Rose Maher
	Sal Sharah
	Wendy Strehlow

Director and Producer, David Williams
Dramaturg, Paul Dwyer
Lighting Designer, Richard Manner
Sound Designer, Gail Priest
Set and Costume Designer, Isabel Hudson
Production Manager, Emma Bedford
Stage Manager, Patrick Howard

CHARACTERS

INTERVIEWER
CONSULTANT PHYSICIAN, female
EXPERIENCED NURSE, female
CONSULTANT SURGEON, male
GP, female
GP ACADEMIC, female
NURSE ACADEMIC, female
CONSULTANT, male
RETIRED CONSULTANT, male
YOUNG DOCTOR, female
REGISTRAR 1, male
REGISTRAR 2, male
INTERN, female
MEDICAL STUDENT, female
NURSE PARAMEDIC, male
FORMER SURGEON, female
HOSPITAL MANAGER, male
SENIOR NURSE, female
NURSE RESEARCHER, male

All actors play multiple roles. Suggested doubling (for a cast of four):

Actor 1: CONSULTANT PHYSICIAN / NURSE ACADEMIC / MEDICAL STUDENT

Actor 2: EXPERIENCED NURSE / CONSULTANT SURGEON / CONSULTANT / RETIRED CONSULTANT / REGISTRAR 2 / HOSPITAL MANAGER

Actor 3: GP / GP ACADEMIC / SENIOR NURSE

Actor 4: YOUNG DOCTOR / REGISTRAR 1 / INTERN / NURSE PARAMEDIC / FORMER SURGEON / NURSE RESEARCHER

The INTERVIEWER role is shared among the actors as required.

NOTES ON TEXT

…	indicates a sentence that trails off and remains unfinished
/	indicates a 'latch'—an interruption that continues immediately from previous speaker
[*Beat*]	indicates a wait time of approximately 3 counts
[*Pause*]	indicates a wait time of approximately 5 counts

This play went to press before the end of rehearsals and may differ from the play as performed.

PART ONE: INTRODUCTIONS

CONSULTANT PHYSICIAN: First of all, I finished, so I've survived, I've made it and it's over.

Pause.

YOUNG DOCTOR: Well, I think I've, for now, left medicine as a career option.

CONSULTANT PHYSICIAN: So the trauma is finished now and I have a psychologist and he calls it the trauma of training.

Laughs.

YOUNG DOCTOR: I may come back to it but I think that's unlikely.

CONSULTANT PHYSICIAN: Now that it's done and I've worked through it I'm okay with it.

GP: I guess, really, it makes sense to say I went straight from school to medicine, which was not uncommon in those days.

CONSULTANT SURGEON: All you needed in my day to be a doctor was to be good at English and science, and I had all that.

GP: There was a lot of focus on the people, the wellbeing of the people.

CONSULTANT SURGEON: It was more about, to be perfectly honest, the opportunity to work for yourself.

GP: I think in our first week they sent us down to visits to the community. They immersed us—the second week we went down a coalmine.

CONSULTANT SURGEON: So as a doctor you could work for yourself. You could run a small business.

GP: Anyway, we went two kilometres under the ground and walked under the water.

CONSULTANT SURGEON: I had some experience of working part-time in a small business.

GP: There was seawater dripping on us in the dark and the dirt.

CONSULTANT SURGEON: That small business that I worked part-time in, was a butcher shop.

Laughs.

INTERN: I think often people want a beautiful story about finding a bird with a broken wing in a park and nursing it back to health, but I don't have one of those.

Laughs.

It's true. But no, I think I just realised that—yeah, I wasn't somebody who wanted to be a doctor from when I was a kid. I wanted to be an archaeologist, actually.

EXPERIENCED NURSE: I recently found—I've moved house quite a bit and recently found something I wrote when I was in Grade Two and it says, 'When I grow up I want to be a nurse'—so I think it's, I want to be a nurse so I can save people's lives. Work with people and save people's life. It's from Year Two.

INTERN: I'm still quite interested in archaeology. I like it.

GP ACADEMIC: [*to* NURSE ACADEMIC] Don't look at me, I never had a penny-drop moment. I said to my mother, 'I think I'd like to do nursing', and she said, 'Don't be ridiculous, you're too smart to be a nurse', no offence. /

NURSE ACADEMIC: [*to* GP ACADEMIC] Lots of offence taken. /

GP ACADEMIC: 'You're too—you have to be a doctor.' From then on it was, like, no choice, that's what I was doing, as far as she was concerned. Any other suggestion was, 'No, no, do medicine'. So sorry, no penny-drops. [*To* NURSE ACADEMIC] Did you take offence?

NURSE ACADEMIC: No, not really. I didn't start off at all wanting to be a nurse and my family situation is completely different. My family had very few hopes for me other than to marry somebody who had a job. So when I talked about wanting to do healthcare, my parents' response to that was something along the lines of, 'Why would you do that? What would be the point?' I wanted a general healthcare degree just to see where I wanted to go with that. So I ended up training in nursing and eventually my interest took me more towards health sociology. It's funny because I get pitched as a nurse but in my mind— /

GP ACADEMIC: You're a sociologist?

NURSE ACADEMIC: Definitely.

GP ACADEMIC: That's interesting.

FORMER SURGEON: I think it's ludicrous to expect a sixteen/seventeen-year-old who can't tell their arse from their head to go, 'This is what I want to do for the rest of my life'.

SENIOR NURSE: I was driven from—I think my mum said I was the age of five and said I was going to be a nurse.

FORMER SURGEON: I had a parent who had a really life-threatening accident throughout my childhood and that put this image in my head about doctors save lives and they're great blah, blah, blah.

SENIOR NURSE: I was one of those. I don't know if we have many of those anymore. But it really was a vocation for me.

FORMER SURGEON: I said, 'Look at the impact that doctors can make'.

SENIOR NURSE: I didn't ever consider throughout school that I was ever going to do anything else.

FORMER SURGEON: There was the dumbest decision I made in my life.

SENIOR NURSE: I know, weird. It was never an option that I was ever going to do anything else. I was very, very focused on that. And very focused on—

A phone rings.

INTERVIEWER: If you need to grab it, that's fine, that's no worries at all.

SENIOR NURSE: Let me just see—it's my son. I'm so sorry.

INTERVIEWER: Oh, talk to your son. I'll turn this off.

Pause.

Okay, we're back on. We were talking about 'yes, from a very early age'.

SENIOR NURSE: I've always been a nurse, I've only recently come into academia so I've been working in the clinical field for over thirty years, including my training, which was a hospital training. I think I've seen many things over the years. I've seen many changes as well, and improvements. I can't say it's all bad. There had been headway in recent years I think. But we still have an issue.

YOUNG DOCTOR: Well, I think I've, for now, left medicine as a career option. I didn't leave because of the culture or because of feeling persecuted personally. However, the culture was certainly not a reason to stay in the profession. There is a light at the end of the tunnel when you're a qualified specialist, but for someone in my position, that's possibly almost a decade down the track, and for me, it's not worth, yeah, not worth continuing with that.

Beat.

I just, I don't think it's worth it.

HOSPITAL MANAGER: I remember being interviewed and I got asked, 'Now you do realise that nursing is not glamorous?' So, okay. All I could think of was saying, 'Yeah, I know I have to empty bedpans and stuff like that. Yep, okay.' The next question was, 'How do you feel about taking direction from a woman?'

Beat.

My immediate response was, 'Well, I've lived with my mother since I was born. I don't answer her back.'

Beat.

I had always envisaged at the end of my training that I was going to do cardiology nursing, and run around with a defib trolley. Save lives. The glamour of it all, even though I was told nursing wasn't glamorous. I ended up doing my paediatric training. And absolutely fell in love.

NURSE PARAMEDIC: My dad is actually a fireman. My mum's a registered nurse. So I was around that environment of shift work, and action, and stories. I just loved listening about them. So I joined the ambulance service, and I worked with them for about six years, full-time. Then went part-time and I did my nursing. I didn't want to do ambulance forever, because I was seeing what was happening to my colleagues. I was seeing what was happening to me. So then I decided to study nursing.

INTERVIEWER: So you're still doing some ambulance work?

NURSE PARAMEDIC: I am, yeah, on a casual basis now. So just work on my days off.

INTERVIEWER: 'I work on my days off.'

NURSE PARAMEDIC: Pretty much, yeah. But I love it. I love getting on a road and driving around. Being a lunatic and putting the sirens on, and turn the music up. Dealing with really sick patients, car accidents and things like that. I love that energy, and I love being there for patients. But I wouldn't want to do it every day.

CONSULTANT PHYSICIAN: I loved it.

EXPERIENCED NURSE: I love nursing. /

CONSULTANT PHYSICIAN: I loved being able to go and talk to patients. /

EXPERIENCED NURSE: And so much—it's not just the physical hands-on. /

CONSULTANT PHYSICIAN: And it felt like a huge privilege that somebody you had just met was prepared to tell you their most intimate details. /

EXPERIENCED NURSE: I've worked with brilliant teams.

CONSULTANT PHYSICIAN: There was a bit of imposter syndrome that goes on, and here are these people spilling, telling you everything.

EXPERIENCED NURSE: Still in contact with a lot of my doctor friends.

CONSULTANT PHYSICIAN: So it was an amazing experience.

EXPERIENCED NURSE: So that sort of—some places I've worked, there hasn't been that segregation of—you're in that pigeonhole and you're in that pigeonhole. It's no, we're a team and we work together.

CONSULTANT PHYSICIAN: It really opens your eyes to the world

EXPERIENCED NURSE: So yeah, so that's—you know.

CONSULTANT PHYSICIAN: So it's an amazing experience.

Pause.

PART TWO: FIRST EXPERIENCES

HOSPITAL MANAGER: So, my first ward placement was quite intense. I think I'd only been in the ward for a week, and I had to lay out my first body, which was really unsettling. I was seventeen when I started nursing, and seventeen and laying out a body of a person I'd met the day before and looked after.

INTERVIEWER: Laying out means preparing the body for going to the morgue?

HOSPITAL MANAGER: Yeah, to go down to the morgue. So, it was to wash the body. I was actually with the third-year nurse who was brilliant. She just talked to me during the whole thing, and would talk to the patient. At first, I was a bit put out by that. I was like, the patient's dead, they can't hear you. She talked about being respectful of the fact that even though this person's life had ended, I'm sure they wouldn't want to hear us talking about what we did on Saturday night at the nightclub. It's more about keeping it respectful.

Beat.

But I struggled with the fact that the practice at the time was, with a black marker, to write their medical record number on their leg. I just found—I really struggled with that and it stuck with me throughout my whole career because it just felt almost a bit meat markety. You know, there's your number and off you go, sort of scenario.

Beat.

NURSE PARAMEDIC: The first day I went on road as a paramedic I still remember getting to a patient and there was a senior ambulance manager there and he goes, 'Quickly, come in'. I was, 'Okay'. I went in, and this patient is dead on the floor. I had not connected that the patient was dead. I was looking at them, 'Oh, are they having a hypo?' Which is a low-level of sugar. I don't know what's going— and he goes, 'Start CPR'. I was, 'Oh, okay'.

Beat.

I jumped on it, and I'd never done CPR before in my life. He's, 'Okay, slow down', because I was going a jack hammer. You know what I mean? Everything was happening at once. He's right, 'Now charge it up'. The machine? I was, 'Oh shit, where's the button to charge it?' I'd been taught all this stuff, but it all went out the window. After that, I had no idea what was happening. I got to the hospital, the patient lived. It was all great. But my head was still back at the house, dealing with what I saw. I was thinking about the eyes of the patient. When they're dead their eyes glaze over like a dead fish pretty much. That had been out for too long. I thought, 'Oh, that's a weird look'.

Beat.

Such a great—well for me it was, probably not for everyone. But for me, I love a good slap in the face sometimes. 'Alright, let's get going.' I remember going home, and I was still living at home with my mum. She goes, 'How was it?' No, I called her after the job. 'How's it going?' 'I just did CPR on someone!' I couldn't get the smile off my face. Might be a bit sadistic, but it's just, I don't know.

Beat.

RETIRED CONSULTANT: This friend of mine, first night on as an intern, and he's doing the after-hours.

NURSE PARAMEDIC: It was the best experience ever.

Beat.

RETIRED CONSULTANT: He got asked by the ward to certify someone as dead. And basically, he got called round there and felt very nervous about getting it right and was worried shitless that he was gonna make a mistake, because he'd never seen a dead body before and so on. Anyway, what he did was, he actually got this mirror that was on the wall and put it straight over the patient's face and was looking for a fog mark on the mirror to see whether the patient was breathing.

Laughs.

And when there was no fog mark on the mirror, he was happy to certify the patient deceased. And the ward staff came in to find this guy holding the mirror over the person's face. Anyway. He became a very good doctor. He became a very good doctor. You, you, yeah, you learnt—I don't think I've, I don't think I've ever had to, you know, I was never trained to certify someone as dead. I was a bit more confident about …

CONSULTANT PHYSICIAN: I was in a country hospital, and it was three o'clock in the morning.

RETIRED CONSULTANT: I didn't need the mirror. If you know what I mean.

CONSULTANT PHYSICIAN: There was me covering the whole hospital, because that's what happens in country hospitals. There's no interns at nights.

The junior anaesthetics registrar, who'd been an anaesthetics registrar for about two minutes, and me, who was in my second year—thank God—as a registrar came up on—we were walking down the corridor together literally chatting and having a cup of tea because there'd been one of those quiet moments—when we walked past a patient who was, oh, looked pretty dead to me. I was like, 'Shit'. So we hit the red button …

Laughs.

… and then we realised we were it.

Laughs.

'Oh fuck, okay. Right, we've got this.' Not dead, pretty close, not dead. Okay, good. Resus, go. Nurses come screaming around with the crash trolley, pads on. We're doing CPR and I'm like, 'Quick, pads on, see what the rhythm is'. Okay, this is a shockable rhythm, I think, 'Is it a shockable rhythm? Shit, I can't remember, I don't know, is it a shockable rhythm?' He's like, 'Yes', I'm like, 'Yes it is, okay, okay, okay'. It's three o'clock in the morning, I can't quite remember, but 'Yes it is, okay, shock'. Bam, okay, adrenaline. So we're going CPR, adrenaline, shocking. Then I'm like, 'I think we need to tube this patient'. He's like, 'I can't tube them'. I'm like, 'You're the anaesthetics registrar, you have to tube them'. He's like, 'I can't'. I was like, 'Okay, just bag and mask'. He has the bag, he was like, 'Okay'. He, he's bagging and masking. We get the patient's rhythm stabilised and we're giving drugs to get the blood pressure up and the patient's unconscious but alive. So I'm standing there and the nurses are just doing their thing—because there's always senior nurses on and the nurses know what they're doing—they're tidying things up. Then there's this pause of, what now? I've got an anaesthetic registrar who can't tube the patient, the intensive care unit's over there and we don't have the drugs, nor do we have anyone in the intensive care unit who can manage this, this has got to be me. And I'm like, 'Next step is, call for help'. So you call the senior person and it's So-and-So and he's like, 'What do you want?' 'Doctor So-and-So, I need you in room blah-blah-blah, there's been an arrest'. He's like, 'Just take them to ICU', and he hangs up on me.

Laughs.

I'm like, 'What do you mean?'

Knocks.

Doctor So-and-So—he's like, 'What?' I was like, 'You need to come and intubate the patient because the anaesthetic registrar doesn't feel confident to'. He's like, 'Don't need to intubate every unconscious patient, just bag and mask them', and he hangs up. I'm thinking, 'What, bag and mask him until morning?' Like, I don't think so. 'Doctor So-and-So, if you don't come and intubate this patient right now I'm calling the director of the hospital.'

Laughs.

He was there in ten minutes. 'Thank you.' He was like, 'Tee-hee-hee, want a cup of tea?' I was like—he thought it was funny because he was always coming.

Laughs.

He thought it was funny just to rile us up a bit. Anyway, the patient got intubated, stabilised in ICU, and everything was fine.

Laughs.

Beat.

Check your own pulse, you know. First rule of arrests is check your own pulse.

Laughs.

It was pretty funny, afterwards. Anyway, the anaesthetic registrar and I had a cup of coffee, the same cup of coffee about three hours later.

We were just like, 'Oh. Biscuit? Did you eat dinner tonight? No. Me neither, another biscuit?'

Pause.

CONSULTANT: I remember the first—I mean this is just—the first baby I delivered, shot out. We had to catch it in slips. It wasn't just easing out. It went …

Makes a flying sound.

I'd got it before it hit the ground, but that was just being prepared to be able to react.

Pause.

I think a lot of people would be horrified to see someone opened up, but when you're doing it, it's—I know personally and I think for others—it's a feeling of—how do you describe it? But you're not dealing with a mess. You're dealing with something important and good, but it's not horrifying. It's quite normal.

PART THREE: THE SYSTEM

SENIOR NURSE: When I was eighteen I left school, and went straight into nursing. It was hospital-based training. This was 1983. It was a culture of—a very hierarchical culture within the nursing profession at that time, and also medicine of course. You were seen and not heard. You didn't have a voice; your opinion was not required, thank you. You did as you were told and if you didn't there were consequences for that. Those consequences would be probably through humiliation, being shouted at in a ward, in the middle of the ward in front of patients, in front of other staff members. You toed the line and you didn't question, no questioning. You stood up when your superiors entered the room. You didn't cross your arms; I got slapped for that once, physically slapped. Slapped across the arm because I did that in front of a sister.

Beat.

But I loved it, which is weird.

Beat.

I think that people can still be very confused about what a nurse's role is. Medical staff are very confused about what a nurse's role is. I think many of them don't appreciate that we actually have a different role to them.

Beat.

I really feel like nursing is about human experience.

INTERN: I'm in my intern year now and I have been saved so many times by the nurses.

SENIOR NURSE: When you try and explain what is the difference between medicine and nursing to anyone, there can still be this sort of conception that we're there to help doctors with their job, and that's really not what I see nursing as at all.

INTERN: Like I remember one time I was sitting in the café and I get a call and one of the nurses says, 'Did you mean to write one point five milligrams?' I was like, 'No'.

SENIOR NURSE: I see my job is helping patients, not helping doctors.

INTERN: So that's essentially a homeopathic dose. Like, there's no way that's going to do anything, and that— /

SENIOR NURSE: We're there to work as a team, but predominately my focus is what helps the patient.

INTERN: Yeah, so she actually brought the medication form to the café and got me to change it.

SENIOR NURSE: It is about human experiences, and it's about helping people with the experience of being ill.

INTERN: It was very sweet.

SENIOR NURSE: That's your job.

INTERN: But they—you know, 'Did you mean to prescribe this?'

SENIOR NURSE: It's how we work through that with patients, how we can enable them to live with that illness or to get over that illness or whatever it may be, that's what a nurse's job is.

INTERN: Or 'Did you know that your patient's respiratory rate is thirty and you should probably be there right now?'

MEDICAL STUDENT: [*to* INTERN] 'Were you planning on killing this person today or would you like—'

Laughs.

Beat.

CONSULTANT SURGEON: My experience in the system meant that I'd seen stuff happening all the way along. Right back to medical student days.

GP: In those days there was—women were still a minority group there.

CONSULTANT SURGEON: I think most of the places that I'd been in the definitive years of my time, were pretty reasonable.

GP: That probably coloured a lot of what happened to me there. /

CONSULTANT SURGEON: But it took me a long time to think about things that I'd seen. /

GP: I mean a lot of good things.

CONSULTANT SURGEON: But when we were fifth-year medical students, the fact that one of the girls in the group slept with one of the lecturers and seemed okay about it. /

GP: I mean it's not all bad. /

CONSULTANT SURGEON: I didn't think too much about that. /

GP: I mean there were a lot of really good things there. /

CONSULTANT SURGEON: But I now recognise that that was probably from his point of view, repeated behaviour— /

GP: But, I guess, talking some of the stories that resonate as far as the culture— /

CONSULTANT SURGEON: And there was a significant power differential there.

GP: For example, I still remember being on the big ward rounds, which are very hierarchical and very—I was young still and quite intimidated really by these huge important people. They kept referring to this person: 'We'll get the social worker to do that, get the social worker to do that'. I'm thinking, 'Oh, that's interesting. I didn't know we had a social worker in our team.' I'm going, 'Oh, they mean me'.

Laughs.

CONSULTANT SURGEON: In terms of female colleagues— /

GP: These are the sort of things you go, 'Oh, I think, oh, that's right, they're getting the female social worker'.

CONSULTANT SURGEON: I think I was aware that it was probably a bit harder for them to do surgery. /

GP: Very, very early on I was being very much put in my place. /

CONSULTANT SURGEON: But reasons weren't necessarily obvious.

GP: I was female, and that was making—they were making that very clear to me that was my position.

CONSULTANT SURGEON: I didn't find any particular issues with my training.

GP: Then I had to stop and go, 'Well, actually, I have to play that system'.

'I have to be the person that—' And you know what? Sorry, orthopaedic surgeon—picking on orthopaedic surgeons—but I know if you wanted to be an orthopaedic surgeon you had to go down on a Friday night and you had to get absolutely pissed—ruggers and beer. How do women break into that culture? Not that I wanted to be an orthopaedic surgeon. It wasn't an area—I never was passionate about that—but it's just that it was a man's world. Certainly, other areas weren't. I mean paediatrics, cardiology, were not that same rugger bugger kind of—you've got to get drunk on a Friday night with all the mates to get in the system. It just—to me, I guess, it was a deliberate choice to go, 'I don't want to play that system. I don't want to be part of a system that doesn't—that does that.'

Pause.

CONSULTANT PHYSICIAN: So have you understood how the system works yet?

Beat.

Right. So in the hospital there's, let's say there's ten teams, all of different specialties. So let's say I'm working for the respiratory department and my patient who's in hospital with pneumonia also turns out to have a gangrenous toe and you think, 'Oh dear, might get a vascular surgeon to look at that.' The way the system works is the intern on the respiratory team rings the registrar on the vascular team to ask that registrar to see the patient and then bring their boss around to give advice on that patient. So that's how the consult system works. So when you do a ward round with your respiratory team in the morning and you see your twenty patients you probably generate five consults to different teams to do for the day.

GP: An intern's role is very clerical. You run around getting everything organised.

REGISTRAR 1: When you're an intern, you're at the lowest part—the lowest rank of this hierarchy—the intern, resident, then registrar, advanced trainee, and then consultant. You're in your mid-twenties, when we became interns, and at that time we've had two degrees, we've worked part-time jobs, we've done—we've proved our intelligence and our role in society, I guess, in a way. Then you feel like you're this subservient little intern at the bottom of the rung.

CONSULTANT PHYSICIAN: So the interns who probably didn't really understand the purpose of the consult in the first place because it was said so quickly on the ward round has to ring a senior vascular registrar who's got a pager— /

REGISTRAR 1: Getting paged all the time.

CONSULTANT PHYSICIAN: The pager goes off— /

REGISTRAR 1: You get pages a thousand times /

CONSULTANT PHYSICIAN: And it's probably the third time that two-minute period that that pager's gone off.

REGISTRAR 1: What am I going to do about it?

CONSULTANT PHYSICIAN: He's probably in the middle of trying to scrub up to do the surgery, he's probably just had his boss yell at him, he's got two interns ringing him and saying our vascular patients are having these problems.

REGISTRAR 1: I think we're all struggling.

CONSULTANT PHYSICIAN: Emergency Department's probably calling him to come down and see the three patients that are waiting to be admitted under vascular surgery—'Where are you?'

REGISTRAR 1: Registrars are struggling, interns are struggling—everyone's struggling.

CONSULTANT PHYSICIAN: The clinic nurses are ringing him because clinic started two hours ago, 'Why haven't you finished that emergency case yet?'

REGISTRAR 1: So if someone takes a break, like, why isn't the work done?

CONSULTANT PHYSICIAN: So when he picks up the phone to the respiratory intern and goes, 'What do you want?', and the respiratory intern goes, 'Oh, I need a—I was wondering if you could see—', he goes, 'Oh, tell me the name, tell me the number. You're an idiot, why don't you even know X, Y and Z?' The respiratory intern who's been there for two weeks doesn't know what any of those words mean, doesn't know what he really wanted to know and gets barked at down the phone and hangs up the phone and bursts into tears, but you can't burst into tears.

SENIOR NURSE: Don't complain, don't say that you can't deal with this because that will be your label, somebody who is—you have to be a coper, you have to be somebody who can deal with all situations and not cry and not get upset or let it affect you.

　　　Pause.

I've always felt that I have been able to work more easily with senior doctors than I am with the junior ones. The junior ones are very quick to dismiss me, they're dismissing you because they just see that they are above you in the pecking order and you are white noise.

NURSE RESEARCHER: Actually, they're in their own pecking order.

SENIOR NURSE: Well, that's right, they're at the bottom of the pecking order when it comes to the medical pecking order, which is a way more defined pecking order than we have in nursing, I think. Maybe it's because they see, 'Okay, well I'm at the bottom of this pile, but I'm certainly above you. My voice is above yours because I'm medicine and you're nursing.' Now, the fact that you've just started in medicine and have been here for five minutes and I've been a nurse for thirty-three years doesn't apply. But they soon learn, I think, when they've been in the system.

Laughs.

NURSE RESEARCHER: I think what it is, because I think the thing I find is they don't pay—you won't get attention by virtue of your role.

SENIOR NURSE: No.

NURSE RESEARCHER: Being a nurse isn't enough to get— /

SENIOR NURSE: That's right.

NURSE RESEARCHER: Where we actually get attention, and that's what senior nurses actually accomplish, is that they know people.

SENIOR NURSE: Yes.

NURSE RESEARCHER: Often what senior nurses know is senior doctors.

SENIOR NURSE: Yes, correct.

NURSE RESEARCHER: So when the intern or the registrar says something you're like, okay, I'm just going to mention that to the consultant that I've known for five years and just check on that, or they know the registrars. It's actually the personal relationships that you establish.

SENIOR NURSE: It's only experienced nurses who have the confidence to be able to do that and to actually—'I don't actually give a shit who I upset anymore', [*laughs*] or even worry about the fact that there's this pecking order going on, 'I don't care'. But when I was a new grad, or probably for the first ten years of my career, of course I had to fit into that system and I would have just not questioned any of that that was being asked of me. If they were asking me to clear up their mess after them or whatever, I probably would have done it.

NURSE RESEARCHER: Yeah. There's this great thing about doctors not being able to— /

SENIOR NURSE: Well, they don't even ask, they just leave it there and I would have just cleaned up after them.

Pause.

CONSULTANT PHYSICIAN: There were some registrars who were just mean. Made you feel stupid—public humiliation was the norm. 'Oh, what do you mean you don't know what?' So there was a whole lot of that sort of thing.But once upon a time I was extremely resilient and it didn't bother me. It was water off a duck's back because I just thought, 'Oh well, that's his problem. I'm here to learn, if he's going to be mean to me that's fine, I'll go ask someone else.' It wasn't until much later that it really started to get to me, and by much later I really mean nearly ten years later. So you can go through—humans can tolerate a lot until they can't.

Laughs.

Pause.

YOUNG DOCTOR: The morning meetings, the morning meetings. So, in orthopaedics we had ward round six-thirty until seven and then trauma meeting at seven. So that's where any patient that's come in overnight gets presented to all of the consultants, each team goes through their list with an update. So it goes from seven until seven-thirty. Those meetings, oh my goodness. All the residents sit across the side wall because we're not important, that's fine; so we sit across the side wall and then all of the registrars would just get hammered, absolutely hammered every morning. They've put up an X-ray and they'd be like, 'This is a person that's come in with this, this is what I've done, this is the plan'. Then every consultant would just go to town and be like, 'What type of fracture is that?' 'No, you're wrong.' Next in the list: 'What type of fracture is that?' 'No, you're wrong.' 'What would you do with that?' Next. Next, next, next. Every morning. I don't know how they all survived it.

CONSULTANT PHYSICIAN: So there was one occasion where I yelled at a registrar, an equal, which is unheard of.

YOUNG DOCTOR: They just get absolutely, just ripped to shreds.

CONSULTANT PHYSICIAN: Because it's much easier to yell at someone who's a junior over the phone because they've got no way to hold you to account.

YOUNG DOCTOR: People do get right answers in the morning meetings and then they just follow up; they follow up with questions until you get a wrong one.

CONSULTANT PHYSICIAN: They can't complain about you to your seniors because if they did that would be, you know.

YOUNG DOCTOR: Yeah. Yep, and then when you get it wrong, it goes to the next one.

CONSULTANT PHYSICIAN: So bad behaviour is protected because I guess I knew that no-one was ever going to pull me up on it.

YOUNG DOCTOR: I know, it's so sad.

CONSULTANT PHYSICIAN: Isn't that terrible? But that's how it happens, because people are under such intense pressure and there's no recourse for bad behaviour.

YOUNG DOCTOR: I'm trying to think if anyone was actually ever praised.

Beat.

REGISTRAR 2: There's this story, this cardiology consultant, who at the end of the term saw the resident, was like, 'Oh, are you the physiotherapist?' The resident was like, 'No, no, I'm your resident. I've been working with you for ten weeks.'

Beat.

REGISTRAR 1: The consultant—when you're an intern, the consultant might ask your registrar, the guy above you, about how the intern is doing, and go— /

REGISTRAR 2: So the intern scurries around for an entire term, trying to please the registrar, hoping for that one second of, 'He's okay'.

REGISTRAR 1:Yeah.

REGISTRAR 2: The thing about this praise we seek and this validation, is just a pat on the shoulder, 'You're okay, mate'. That could light up an intern's week.

REGISTRAR 1: That could last through the week.

REGISTRAR 2: That could get you through a whole week. It's just like, 'Oh, great'. It's quite... So it's disastrous.

CONSULTANT PHYSICIAN: So I was very mindful not to be mean to interns because I remembered what it felt like and I always would if they got it completely wrong, I probably said, 'Hey, I'm going to stop you there. These are the—' Instead of making them guess— 'These are the five things I need every time you call. Do you mind going away and calling back in ten minutes with these five things? Thanks very much, see you later.'

Beat.

I think I did well until right at the end when I was over the peak myself, completely burnt out and angry, I was mean to everybody. I was behaving in a way that I thought I never would. Yeah, it was no different—this sounds terrible—but it was no different to what everybody else had been doing.

Laughs.

Not everybody, but it was just—someone would ring you and you'd be in the middle—I was in the middle of—let's not pretend it wasn't me—I was in the middle of clinic and an intern would ring me and it wasn't fast enough for me, it wasn't concise enough. I was busy, I was trying to do a very important conversation with a patient and I would say, 'Can you at least give me the correct name, for God sakes. Look just call me back in five minutes', and I'd hang up. Just short, snappy, belittling I think is the best word for it, and I knew where it'd come from. I'd been belittled by a lot of people throughout my whole training and so you pick up those behaviours.

Pause.

EXPERIENCED NURSE: A patient came in, who—he'd come off his push-bike and he had an accident and he was complaining of hip pain. So straight away—until proven otherwise I'm suspicious of—I want to make sure that person hasn't fractured hips. Because if you then try and log-roll them and you move that unstable fracture, they can haemorrhage. It's a fairly, it's a nice simple test just to see if there's anything there. This doctor, I had to sort of say, 'Oh look, just before we log-roll, he's just complaining a bit of hip pain, do you mind just— would you mind us having a quick look before we roll?' So, I did try that whole graded escalation and it—in the end, I had to say, 'Please don't log-roll until we've checked it. He's got a pelvic binder from the ambulance service. He's complaining of hip pain, can we please just check him before we roll him?' In the middle of this whole room, this doctor just screamed at me, yelled at me, he called me all kinds of names, in a room full of my nursing colleagues and his colleagues. Interestingly, behind the scenes later, his boss was watching from another resus bay and his boss—I saw her pull him aside. I don't know what they said, he didn't tell me. But then his boss came and said, 'Look, you actually did the right thing even though you got screamed at. You actually did the right thing by trying to establish that sort of thing.' Like yeah, but that doesn't exactly help me now does it, when you've had someone yelling and screaming at you across a room in a situation that's high-pressured. For his boss to sort of quietly, behind the scenes to say, 'I felt that you did the right thing', that's nice, and I'm grateful that she did that, but did you say that to the doctor? Did you say that to any of the other six people in the room watching? Or the ambos at the back watching? Anything—the patients in the other bays? So, you think, 'Oh, that's a bit unfair'. But anyway.

Beat.

SENIOR NURSE: What I found very interesting when I went into more senior nursing positions, was as soon as I was out of a uniform I felt medical staff had a different attitude towards me. As soon as you put that uniform back on, it's very symbolic. I was quite surprised by them actually valuing my opinion. Isn't that interesting? Yeah. Obviously, I was in a more senior nursing position. But I was still—you know, one day I had a uniform on, the next day I was in civvies. I felt that all of a sudden, my opinion was valid. Which was a bit surprising for me. I just—it was very distinct. Actually somebody was listening or actually wanted my opinion: 'What do you think?' I'm like, 'Oh, that's interesting, you wouldn't have asked me that when I had my scrubs on'—you know I mean?

Pause.

CONSULTANT: It was built in the system from top to bottom.

YOUNG DOCTOR: Every single day and I was— /

CONSULTANT: For example, just the working hours—you could call that a form of bullying if you like. /

YOUNG DOCTOR: It's just ridiculous. /

CONSULTANT: It was not seen as that. It was seen as normal practice

YOUNG DOCTOR: We get paid from six-thirty in the morning, but six-thirty in the morning is when the ward round starts— /

CONSULTANT: It's what you do, but when I was an intern at a hospital in 1980, we worked eighty hours the first week and a hundred and twenty hours the second week. /

YOUNG DOCTOR: —and part of the intern job is updating all of the patient list and there's twenty to thirty patients. You have to update this list, ready for the ward round.

CONSULTANT: That's not just sitting at a desk. That's on your feet doing it. We were paid for fifty-five hours a week. I remember going to the CEO at the time and saying—with a couple of others, 'Look, we're doing an average of a hundred hours a week. We're being paid for fifty-five. Surely we should be paid for more.' He said, 'Oh no. Well, you're doing so many hours, because you're young and you're so slow—so we can only pay you for what you should be able to do in fifty-five hours.' Which was a classical spin, absolute nonsense. But again, this was a person who was non-clinical. He had no idea of what it was actually like to do what the junior doctors did. People in management are—they're very separate from those who are actually hands-on with patients, and the living and dying—part of it—and so they have power over doctors in various ways, but they're quite cut off, really. There's sort of a split, generally speaking, between management and clinical staff.

Pause.

INTERVIEWER: [*to* NURSE PARAMEDIC] You've got this—I'm just saying this because the recorder won't pick it up. But you've got this really cheeky grin— /

NURSE PARAMEDIC: Yeah. /

INTERVIEWER: —as you're talking— /

NURSE PARAMEDIC: Yeah. /

INTERVIEWER: —about management.

NURSE PARAMEDIC: Yeah.

INTERVIEWER: Is there anything behind that?

NURSE PARAMEDIC: Yeah, there is. Yesterday I was triaging patients and there's a whole political issue at the moment about off-loading ambulances. So you could come in, and you might be really unwell. But you came in on an ambulance and you might not be as unwell. But because the government at the moment needs ambulances back on road, they'll give you a bed, and they'll keep you with me without a bed. Despite me voicing my concern. /

INTERVIEWER: So your clinical judgement?

NURSE PARAMEDIC: It goes out the window. Which is very unfortunate.

Beat.

Why I was smiling before is because the manager that I was thinking of, doesn't necessarily have that clinical skill anymore. But was letting me know about what was actually going to happen for the disposition of the patients. I've never really disagreed with anyone, and I let them know that I don't agree with them. I'm not a confrontational person, but I found that quite interesting. Last night when I was home I was, 'Wow; this world is crazy'. It's all because of political things that I'm not really used to. It's very stressful sometimes, having to have those arguments with people to say this patient is a lot sicker. 'Wait, I need to stop, I'm just going to finish this and then we're going to have a chat about that.' Then before I knew it the decision had already been made. The ambulance patient had moved to the bed. My sick patient still was sitting with me.

Pause.

EXPERIENCED NURSE: So, it was a twelve-and-a-half-hour shift. So, I got there early because I'm still old school. I went into the tearoom before we even began and I sat down with a book and think, 'Oh, peace and quiet. Yeah, I've got fifteen minutes with a book, yeah.' I went in there and there were these two guys talking. The first guy, big guy, like half-sleeve tatts, muscly, big tall nuggetty guy, standing up, and he's sort of shaking his head with his hands on his hips. Like body totally deflated. He was chatting to another guy and just like, 'I just don't know, I just don't see a way out of this. I can't stay here, like I just can't keep staying here and working here. It's just so awful.' You know, like he was clearly really—not frustrated, annoyed, like he was clearly distressed and sad and hopeless.

And the other guy's going, 'What about extra study, could you do some study and then you can move out?' 'I can't stay here while I'm studying'. I was just sitting in the room, trying to remember to turn the page so I didn't look obvious.

We all went onto the start of the shift, that was fine. I came back in for my first break. There was another girl chatting to another person. It was more of a matter of fact and—oh, I've already—'I'm going to see, I'm going to see him in my next whenever, when I've got a day off or whatever. I'm not doing this shit anymore. It's just—it's just too much and he's just this—' Anyway. So, same dialogue again about going to see this particular manager and—I thought, 'Right, well that's two out of two breaks'.

Then I went in on my last shift and—my last break, sorry. There was a girl sobbing, 'I can't go back, I can't do this anymore. I'm not doing this.' Like there and then was ready to throw in her entire nursing career. Because really, that's what she was saying, 'I'm just walking off and I'm never coming back'.

I said, 'Oh look, I know I'm nobody, I'm just a casual here, but you're not the first person I've seen doing this, not even on this shift. You're the third person that I've seen this shift who's in this situation. Surely, if you got together maybe as a group.' She's just like, 'No, we've all tried it'. I was just like, 'Oh my gosh, wow, wow'. I've never seen anything quite as hopeless. Like it was just—to use the word hopeless, it was a situation void of hope. It was just like, 'Wow, you're too young to be chucking in your career'. Yeah, it was so confronting. You think, 'Gosh, everybody's just—' It just felt like everything was done out of fear as their motivation. It's like wow, when did fear become a driver as a nurse, that's awful. That's just awful.

Pause.

INTERN: I was actually recently thinking about one of the medical students that I started out with who was a perfectly lovely person. I mean, they still are a lovely person, but I remember when he was an intern and having a chat to him. He was saying that he thought—he was talking about the reaction against bullying in medicine and saying that it was a shame because we may have less suicides but we'll have worse doctors.

Beat.

So, yeah.

Pause.

PART FOUR: POWER

CONSULTANT SURGEON: I remember a time when I was qualified but was just completing my time and we agreed that we'd do these two operations. I arranged with the consultant that we'd do them on the Saturday morning. So we were all there at eight o'clock on a Saturday morning and the anaesthetist was ready to go. We got to ten past eight and there was no sign of this surgeon who was normally punctual. I was allowed to operate in my own right. So the anaesthetist said to me, 'Well, why don't we just get on with it?' The staff are: 'Sure, let's get on with it'. I'm fine: 'Let's do it'. I've got the first operation finished forty minutes later, five to nine. He comes storming through the doors. He says, 'What are you fucking doing. You know you're not allowed to do these fucking cases on your fucking own', and all of that. Everybody was a bit surprised. I said, 'Well, we've got another one to do, do you want to do that one or shall I do that one?' He said, 'No, you do that one and I'm going to watch you'. I said, 'Okay, that's fine'. So we did that and it all went well. Then we went outside and we went back to the change rooms. The power differential was modest. He was actually only two or three years qualified. I was now qualified. So I slammed the door. I repeated the dose in reverse about what I thought of him and his behaviour in the operating room. We parted friends, interestingly. Our careers have overlapped and inter-sected on and off since and there's been no problem at all.

> *Beat.*

FORMER SURGEON: I guess the pressure does bring out the worst in people, but it's the culture that allows it to happen.

> *Beat.*

CONSULTANT SURGEON: His career's turned out pretty well, and mine's turned out pretty well.

> *Beat.*

FORMER SURGEON: It's usually things like—I mean, it is personal experiences, but it will be things like: 'What are you doing?' In the context of a patient hearing everything that's going on in an operating room or 'Don't worry, you're no more pathetic than your predecessors'. There will be things like not even acknowledging the fact that you have a name. One of the classic lines I would get was 'woman'. That was from obviously male seniors. Women to women in the operating room I haven't had that experience. It's always been from the male seniors saying things like, 'Yeah, woman, are you blind?' The patient can hear everything. There's been situations where the patient's come up to you afterwards and they're like, 'Are you okay?' Or 'I can't believe he just treated you that way'. Sometimes it makes you sort of doubt your abilities. I've had them ask, 'Am I the first person you're operating on?' It's just that humiliating even though they're the hundredth whatever that you're doing that procedure on but because there's just so much noise getting made in the operating room that they have no faith or confidence in you. Yeah, it's—I've personally experienced it almost always in front of other people, including nurses, including other doctors. They'll come up to you afterwards and say, 'Are you okay?'

Beat.

CONSULTANT: When I was a medical student, you do your rounds and the surgeons choose who's there at the bedside.

Beat.

FORMER SURGEON: They will never step in and say, 'What's going on here? Don't treat her that way.' Everyone just shuts up, puts up.

Beat.

CONSULTANT: There was a patient who had a neurological problem and he said, 'Well, what's wrong with this man?' 'You, you, you, you.' I said, 'He has got a lesion in the caudate nucleus'.

INTERVIEWER: Lesion in the …?

CONSULTANT: The caudate nucleus, which is a central part of the brain. He nearly fell over. He said, 'How can you know that? You can't possibly know that.' Now, the only reason I knew it was because I'd been reading about it the night before. I wasn't particularly brilliantly knowledgeable in this. I just happened to have read about it. So at the end of the tutorial he said, 'Why don't you come and help me in theatre?' I thought, 'Oh well, a chance to learn something'. Alright, so I went in there and we were doing an abdominal operation and he's doing the actual surgery and I'm holding something open. Then he says, 'Now you repeat after me: Doctor So-and-So is the greatest surgeon who ever lived'. I'm thinking, 'What? You're joking.' No, he wasn't. 'No, come on. You repeat after me: Doctor So-and-So is the greatest surgeon who ever lived.' All the nurses' eyes were rolling.

NURSE ACADEMIC: I actually hate hospitals.

CONSULTANT: Then he said it a third time. Now, this is a fact. I'm not making this up. This literally happened. I was feeling absolutely furious with this, but all I can do is just stay here, do what has to be done. That's what happened. You could see it in his eyes. He looked like a psychopath, if you can say that. He had these eyes that were—well, diabolical—if you like, to not be too florid about it. That's one of the most memorable things I've ever experienced.

Pause.

NURSE ACADEMIC: My very first placement as a student nurse was in— shall I say the name of the hospital?

INTERVIEWER: We can edit it out later.

NURSE ACADEMIC: It was a private hospital and I worked on this ward and I was actually dealing with a patient with another nurse, who was very good, very professional. This patient had a wound that was not healing. So we were trying to deal with it. She finally says to me, 'Okay, I really, really need help. Can you just go and get support?' I walked out and I remember there was a nurse unit manager, and they kind of run the ward, if you like, and she was speaking with a doctor. They were speaking, speaking, speaking. My colleague is sitting in the other room in a difficult situation having to calm the patient who was getting quite distressed.

I was like, 'Oh'. I just waited for that little pause in the conversation and I said, 'Oh, do you mind, I just need to ask you a question. I'm really sorry to interrupt, I just need to ask you a question. This is happening in the other room, dah, dah, dah', and she just turned around to me and just shouted at me, and what she shouted was, 'Can't you see I'm speaking to the doctor? How dare you interrupt me?' I was just like, 'Fuck', and so I didn't know what to do. I was stuck.

Beat.

I think it was about the hierarchy. I think she felt embarrassed when I'd interrupted.

INTERVIEWER: In front of a doctor?

NURSE ACADEMIC: In front of a doctor, and I think she felt that she needed to assert her power in the ward over me. I really didn't like hospitals after that. Hated hospitals.

Pause.

GP: I did a cardiology term. That was—oh, I think I'd been a doctor for a whole three months by this stage. There were two interns, two of us. The other one was male. There was a Friday meeting where the cardiothoracic surgeons and the cardiologists would meet in a very small, dark room. I would be the one who'd have to make—I'd do a little presentation and then I'd have to show the videos of the angiograms. Of course, the lights went out. The first time it happened I thought, 'Oh, that surgeon is standing awfully close, hmm'. I thought, 'Hmm, I'll just move a little bit this way'.

Beat.

Then the lights go off the next time, I think, and he's standing really close and getting closer. I didn't know what—didn't know how to deal with it. He was a very senior surgeon, very respected at the hospital, and I just basically just kept moving away. The next movie was coming up.

Beat.

I spoke to the other intern, 'I feel really uncomfortable with this guy'. So the intern came and stood—he always put himself between the surgeon and me, which was great, so that solved the problem, but there was no consequences for the surgeon.

Beat.

What was tragic during that term is that other intern, he killed himself—not related to this at all. He suicided during that term, which was hideous from many, many, many levels. From a personal level I was a bit like, 'Oh my God, like I'm really exposed now'. It was very traumatising. He just didn't turn up to work on the Monday basically. So, again, that—and then—I guess I felt then my problem was very small compared to it all.

A long pause.

INTERN: That is something that can't really be justified by a lot of—like a lot of the things that happened in medicine have justifications. Like this woman isn't going to be strong enough to be an orthopaedic surgeon or this woman isn't going to be able to give their time to surgical training. But sexual harassment doesn't really—I think the main justification is just people need to learn to suck it up, which isn't great. But that's something that is perpetuated, I think, by the hierarchical system because when you have middle-aged white men who have grown up in this boys-will-be-boys culture, and men our age to be fair, asking medical students for their numbers and asking them questions about their sex life and 'Show me your back tattoo'. You can't—because of this hierarchy, you can't do anything about it. Because that person controls your grade and they control your progression in the career. Medicine is a very small world, so that person knows everybody else. So if you become a problem, you're blacklisted. You're not just blacklisted for that person, you're blacklisted for everybody.

Beat.

MEDICAL STUDENT: I had a placement with a fairly notorious surgeon, and it was great because he was my supervisor.

INTERN: Yay.

MEDICAL STUDENT: All of my surgical placement and I had some idea of his reputation.

INTERN: Like everybody knew and he was still getting students—sorry, continue.

MEDICAL STUDENT: Yeah, and—no, there'd been already like one complaint, I think.

Laughs.

Yeah, and I was scared. I'm not going to lie. I was really scared. Then all it was just like this pervasive level of regular sexual harassment, but he didn't touch me.

Laughs.

Blocked me out. I was relieved to have only had ten weeks with this person and to find myself not his type. Like that was my—not thinking about just being in surgery with him and his surgery friends, quizzing me about my relationship history and sex life, because I was engaged at the time.

Beat.

They wanted to know about my fiancé. Then once they established that my fiancé was also a medical student who wanted to be a surgeon, what I could possibly have that would have attracted him enough to want to marry me? Like what are you bringing to the table? No-one else is in that room who is conscious. The patients are unconscious and just hours and hours of this bullshit.

Beat.

I was later approached by the hospital because someone else had been persistently propositioned by this person. That person was brave enough to say something about it which I was very impressed about. There was maybe quite a lot of political will I would say at the hospital to actually sort this out. Because this person had this atrocious—not just bad but atrocious reputation for so long and suddenly sexual harassment in the hospital—in hospital systems—is very high profile. 'So, what's been going on? Anything you want to share?' I was like, 'No. Maybe.' It's all such—it's so low-level. You know, all this—like I've got a sheet this long of inappropriate things. But it's not—I don't think it is what you were looking for because what they want is—to do anything and to make any change or move is, well, he touched me here, here, here, and here. Or he said I would get a good grade only if I did these things. Not everyone is an idiot to that extent. It's much more low-level, but just constant. Or it's, 'Why don't you come away with me to my—wherever and whenever?' Then the person says no, and it's like, 'I was just joking'. You know, just like— /

INTERN: Yeah. It's always, 'It was just a joke'.

MEDICAL STUDENT: It wouldn't have been a joke if you'd said yes.

INTERN: Yeah.

Pause.

HOSPITAL MANAGER: You know, I've had a personal experience as a student where there was inappropriate pressure. It was from another nurse that was trying to use their position to get something out of me. It was one that was sexually uncomfortable, but I had a good group of friends that I could discuss it with and get some support. But I certainly couldn't go to the manager, and I wouldn't have gone to the manager because then I would have been branded as having been difficult. Because this individual was seen as a great nurse. That's the other thing. They're often seen as a great nurse, or a great doctor, it doesn't mean they're a great person, unfortunately. They just do their job very well.

Pause.

PART FIVE: CRASH

REGISTRAR 2: My wife's paediatric and she's pretty angry that she's still doing nights and still doing evening shifts. [*Pointing to* REGISTRAR 1] He doesn't do any nights. Neither of us—I do nights—I don't do nights. I'm not supposed to do nights at all.

REGISTRAR 1: I do nights if I feel like it.

REGISTRAR 2: But you should—you're not forced to do it. Most people are forced to do it.

REGISTRAR 1: No. Well, I mean, when I go back into hospital training I will be—I won't be forced to do nights specifically— /

REGISTRAR 2: But on-call— /

REGISTRAR 1: —but I'll be forced to do— /

REGISTRAR 2: But that'll be possibly if you're consulting. /

REGISTRAR 1: —on-call.

REGISTRAR 2: This morning the—we're having a meeting and the palliative care consultant said, 'My registrar had an accident today. She totalled her car on the M5. She—there was an incident on the M5—it was her.' She was on-call last night. She was taking calls every hour. I was just livid—this has happened too many times. I mean, there's lots of stories of surgical residents—I've had a car accident myself, coming home.

REGISTRAR 1: Yeah, tell him about your accident, because that was—that was coming home from a shift, was it?

REGISTRAR 2: Yeah, that was—I, well, I had an accident. /

REGISTRAR 1: Well, I had an accident, driving back from a night shift, and that—I was lucky that I survived that. That was a microsleep, which I didn't anticipate, even though I had done everything I could to try to avoid that. Your one was funny too, because I think it highlights something else.

REGISTRAR 2: I think I was—it was in the first year of my basic physician training. I'd done a night shift. Then—I lived about forty minutes from work, and I made that commute every time. I drove home and then—I was driving. I had a coffee, whatever—you try and do what you can. Then I fell—I was starting to fall asleep. I was swerving. Then, as I was just about—about two hundred metres from my house, I just fell asleep. I swerved and hit a car. It was like, 'What if someone was in that car? What if I hurt someone?' Your blood alcohol is like point oh-four by that stage. It's—you cannot think straight.

REGISTRAR 1: You're saying it's the same as a blood alcohol level of point oh-four. You weren't also drinking.

REGISTRAR 2: No, I wasn't, but yeah.

REGISTRAR 1: Just to clarify. I think you understood that.

REGISTRAR 2: When you're an intern, you're young—you're younger. You're ambitious. You want to impress. You want to—you're a martyr.

REGISTRAR 1: You're still young and you feel invincible.

REGISTRAR 2: You feel unbreakable.

REGISTRAR 1: You're still—you're in your twenties. I mean, interestingly, just on the topic of car accidents, and you say, trying to impress and so forth, you actually had another car accident last year.

REGISTRAR 2: Oh, yeah.

REGISTRAR 1: Remember, it wasn't so much your fault. You were driving on the way to work in the morning. /

REGISTRAR 2: Yeah, that was— /

REGISTRAR 1: Then you had a three-car accident. After something like that, what did he do? He drove into work. He didn't take the day off, he's like, 'I have to go to work. I have to be there for the patients—I have to do the round of patients. I have to impress the bosses. I have to—there's too much happening. They can't survive without me.'

REGISTRAR 2: Who will see the patients?

REGISTRAR 1: Who will see the patients?

REGISTRAR 2: Who will round them?

REGISTRAR 1: Then you came in.

REGISTRAR 2: That's very— /

REGISTRAR 1: That's very common. I mean, the amount of time we've been sick and came into work anyway, because we felt there was no choice.

Beat.

CONSULTANT PHYSICIAN: Once you get into advanced training you're that person on the phone, you're on-call. The hours actually get worse because you do one in three weekends and the weekend starts Friday morning. Because you've got your day job and then you take phone calls around the clock until Monday and then you go to your day job Monday. So there's no days off. During the Saturday and Sunday you will do a ward round, so that might take four hours or it might take eight hours. My experience where I worked was it took ten hours most weekend days. So you'd do a—you'd be up all night on the phone on the Friday, you'd come in, you'd do a ten-hour ward round on the Saturday. Then you'd be up all night on the phone on Saturday and you've come in and you'd do a ten-hour round on Sunday. Then you'd be up all night on the phone on Sunday night and then you'd do your normal work week from Monday on. For me it was mainly transplants, so you'd normally get the organ donor offer at midnight and then you spend two hours working them up, you go in. So you're probably there from midnight until four, or on the phone at least from midnight until four, and then the patient comes into the hospital at six. So you try and get two hours' sleep and then go in at six-thirty. So yeah, that's pretty bad hours.

INTERVIEWER: Would you go into the operating theatre when it's a transplant? Or that's— /

CONSULTANT PHYSICIAN: No, because I'm not a surgeon, so the surgeons have to do that. But they're up all night and then they do surgery.

INTERVIEWER: On two hours' sleep.

CONSULTANT PHYSICIAN: Yeah, commonly, yeah.

INTERVIEWER: Sounds dangerous.

CONSULTANT PHYSICIAN: It's a shocker, it should be illegal. My dad works for, he's a lawyer who works for mining companies, and he says in no other industry would that be allowed. In fact, if a foreman was requesting his mining staff to work those hours there'd be a ministerial enquiry. But the hours are better now for doctors than they used to be so there's this culture of: 'Well, we did it, suck it up, it's not as bad as it used to be'.

INTERVIEWER: The general public would be alarmed.

CONSULTANT PHYSICIAN: Should be, should be alarmed. But they've been told, it's in the papers all the time.

INTERVIEWER: What about the doctors' union? Have they lobbied for safer working hours? Do they have any teeth?

CONSULTANT PHYSICIAN: I'm going to throw that back to you. What gives a union its power?

INTERVIEWER: The members?

CONSULTANT PHYSICIAN: Striking. Ever heard of a doctors' strike?

Beat.

It can't be done because the patients suffer and doctors would prefer that their patients didn't suffer and that they suffered, I think, is one part of it. They would prefer they suffer than their patients suffered. And also everybody's got in their mind that it's a temporary problem. Because once you finish training, you know. You've only got to do this for seven years, it's not forever, so you don't need to fight for your rights because it's going to end soon. So all you've got to do is survive and get out.

Pause.

EXPERIENCED NURSE: I mean, at the end of day, honestly, I do think there's some fundamental things that can't be avoided and money is really the kicker. There is no—like tying funding. But at one point it was that if you don't meet these benchmarks you will lose funding. So, having money tied to these benchmarks— /

INTERVIEWER: Benchmarks such as?

EXPERIENCED NURSE: The four-hour rule. Yeah, the four-hour rule. So, someone who comes in has to be seen and either admitted— /

INTERVIEWER: Triaged or— /

EXPERIENCED NURSE: —or discharged within four hours. A clinical decision has to be made within four hours. /

INTERVIEWER: To reduce waiting times in hospital emergency departments?

EXPERIENCED NURSE: Yes, yes.

INTERVIEWER: But doesn't that just mean people end up in beds in hall corridors and— /

EXPERIENCED NURSE: Or worse still, they get sent home when they shouldn't be sent home because, well, we're going to weigh this up and decide are they clinically at risk or not. There's no beds. It's a low clinical risk, send them home.

INTERVIEWER: So, are you describing to me an audit culture which allows a minister for health to stand up and say something impressive in parliament about how we've managed to get waiting times down?

EXPERIENCED NURSE: Yeah.

INTERVIEWER: So what's the opportunity cost for the minister to stand up and say, 'We've managed to get waiting times down by X', what's the opportunity cost in terms of patient care, do you feel?

EXPERIENCED NURSE: I think it's that the patients don't get care. They might physically have their blood test done. They might physically get their X-ray. They might physically get their script for antibiotics. But if we look at the—if we honestly view human beings—and this—when I first did my training, it's a huge component of our education. A human being is made up of the biological, psychological, the social, the spiritual. All—a human being is all of these components rolled into one.

Beat.

You used to see it on admission forms. The questions like that would be asked, the tick box: 'Does this person—who do they live with and so on'. All of that used to be a part of the assessment when they came in. Then I noticed more and more, those dropped away. They were really only concerned with very specific measurable, tangible, physiological qualities. We didn't have time for the rest of that. We didn't have time. On the old nursing observation forms, there used to be a section where—it was on the front cover, you put their patient sticker on. You write down a whole bunch of information like their next of kin, their allergies. Then there was a little section where they used to ask, 'Does the patient have a religion?' Nobody ever asks that. Nobody ever actually did anything with that, because who's got time for that?

Beat.

I do vividly remember a patient one day who was quite distressed. Now not in an open wailing gnashing-of-teeth kind of distressed, but that you could see this person was silently, quietly, very distressed. They weren't the one pushing the buzzer or anything. There was nothing to draw my attention to this person, but when you looked closely they were crying, solidly, while I was there. I went over and I chatted

to them and I was just—what it boiled down to, they were generally
scared that they were going to die. They weren't going to, but that's
not the point. They were scared that they were going to and they were
scared that that was going to happen before their minister had come
in to chat to them. But things like that I think—the cost of focusing on
money and numbers and less waiting times is—the stories you hear
about.

Pause.

GP: One of the most traumatic events of my life occurred at a country
hospital on an Easter. I was in my first term—or my second term—of
being my second year; so I've been a doctor for thirteen months. This
hospital, being on the highway, every now and then has massive horrible accidents. They had a massive horrible accident, and I was the
doctor for the hospital. I did get warning. They did say there's people
coming and I—because I went into action mode and tried to do everything I could to prepare. I did ring the specialists and say, 'Please
come', but I don't think they really understood how please come— It
was absolute bedlam. It was like being in a war zone.

Even now I think about it. I think I want to cry. I saw people die
who shouldn't have died, because I didn't have the skills or the—it
was a nightmare. I had—I mean, one that still makes me—see, I'm
tearing up straight away: the little two-year-old came in, still in the
car seat, with an obvious fractured head. Then his parents came in,
who had the tops of their—sorry, this is gross if you're not medical.
I went, 'Oh, what's that cloth there for? Oh, his brain. Oh, right. Put
that back.' It was—we're talking—sorry. I won't do too many more
gross things.

It was like being in a war zone. One of them had a hole in their lung
and the lung was basically compressed and they couldn't breathe. I
went, 'Well, I've seen someone put a tube in the lung, I'd better do
that'. So you know, off I'm doing and, of course, this is all happening,
and you're thinking, 'Where is everybody?' The specialists were still
at home, waiting for a second phone call but, of course, I was drowning in blood.

It was thirty-six hours until I stopped, so from—and then I did get air
ambulances and whatever, and I sent people—I think, looking back, I

did as well as I possibly could, but it's a little country town and I was a junior doctor, and I saw children die in front of me. They may have died anyway, but I felt, of course, responsible. It was absolute hell.

In the middle of that we had funny stories—sort of funny when you're medical. In the middle of this, this man arrives at the hospital thinking he's Jesus.

Laughs.

Anyway, in the middle of all that I'm trying to get an ambulance and the police need to send him, to schedule him because, clearly, he needed to be scheduled. I mean, he was funny because he really did think he was Jesus. He was walking around amongst all this bedlam blessing everyone.

Laughs.

It was just like, oh okay—it's sort of funny in a way. Anyway, he then went off in a police car. Alright, he's gone. There's an ambulance and an air ambulance to the Children's Hospital. It was like, ugh.

Thirty-six hours later, and I finally got around to the truck driver who caused all of this, who'd had a fracture. He was quite—he started hitting on me too. I'm thinking, 'You are a pig. You have killed people and you are now trying to crack on to the doctor. This is so inappropriate.'

Beat.

This is not a medical story in a sense because he was—maybe he was in shock. Maybe—whatever. I don't know. Anyway, that's not the story. So it was the whole of Easter.

Beat.

The other doctor—there's two of you—she'd gone home for the weekend and then decided this hospital was all too hard and didn't come back. Amongst all of this I never got relief. Literally the whole of Easter—from—I think, I started Thursday and worked right through, and then—so now I haven't slept—and, again, a horrible medical story. When I get to that point, when I haven't slept for three or four days, I haven't eaten, I actually start vomiting. Sorry, gross, but my body starts shutting down. It starts actually purging itself. I start throwing up.

Beat.

I still remember with—a child came in with severe asthma—I need to get a drip in. The little child—at six o'clock in the morning—and Mum was there, the child's there, and I'm trying to put the drip in. I'm actually just about to get it in and I literally leant over and went blah in the sink. Came back, put the drip in, and the mother's just looking at me, and going, 'I'm really sorry, I'm really sorry. But—' Blah—

Laughs.

Like anyway, so the whole thing was one of my worst experiences of my life.

Beat.

On the Tuesday—so medical admin opens again, by this stage I'm going, 'Where is this other doctor?' I'm ringing up, and they go, 'Oh, she's not coming back'. I said to them, 'I've got to tell you, I'm dangerous. I haven't slept and da-da-da.' I said, 'I can't—I'm telling you that patients are at risk because I am just traumatised beyond belief. I haven't slept. I haven't eaten. I'm just not functioning and you need to do something for the sake of the patients, not necessarily me.' Do you know what they said? 'It will put hairs on your chest.' And I replied, 'I don't actually want hairs on my chest'. I got no support at all from that.

Beat.

I guess the point of the story is then, when you come back in again, to apply for your job for the next year. You come in for an interview, which is usually fairly—just a nothingy kind of interview unless you want to go on one of the specialist training schemes. I didn't. I just wanted to do another general year because I felt that I could get more experience doing general things. I walked into the interview, and there was a very intimidating long table with five very high-level doctors at the table. You're a little bit anxious when you're walking in that door. Before I even crossed to the table where the seat was, they said—one of them said to me, 'Oh, so you're that whinger from that country hospital'.

Beat.

I said, 'Absolutely. Are you aware of what happened when I was there?' That was the final straw for me. That's when I—I can't work in this system. I cannot be part of a system that cares so little. That's when I was going, 'How can you say you're the whinger because I rang and said to you, 'I am dangerous'? And your patients, that you're responsible for, need care and nothing happened. I can't stay in this system.'

A long pause.

PART SIX: AT THE EDGE

CONSULTANT PHYSICIAN: So I drove to The Gap with the intention to jump off about three months into advanced training.

Beat.

I got a phone call from a friend who said, 'Hi, what are you doing?'

Beat.

I said, 'Not much'.

Laughs.

Beat.

He said, 'Do you want to have coffee on Saturday?'

Beat.

'Yeah sure great, okay, great, see you on Saturday.'

Beat.

So I got back into my car and drove home and then I went to work the next day like nothing had happened.

A long pause.

I'm surprised more people don't successfully kill themselves, to be honest.

Beat.

INTERN: So I could tell you— /

CONSULTANT PHYSICIAN: I couldn't figure out how to get out. /

INTERN: So I've had depression for a long time. /

CONSULTANT PHYSICIAN: I couldn't figure out how to make it stop. /

INTERN: And this year, I had moments where I was having suicidal ideation.

CONSULTANT PHYSICIAN: I couldn't figure out how to make the pressure go away.

INTERN: I actually got quite close a few times.

CONSULTANT PHYSICIAN: And quitting wasn't an option.

INTERN: You're aware of the law or the rule around mandatory reporting of mental illness? I can tell you unequivocally now that the fear of mandatory reporting meant that I did not tell my doctor.

CONSULTANT PHYSICIAN: It's crazy to think that quitting would be less of an option than jumping off a cliff, but at the time it seemed like I couldn't let it go, I couldn't give up on everything I had done, but I couldn't keep doing it either. I couldn't face the failure, I couldn't face having given so many years and hours and blood, sweat and tears to then quit.

INTERN: I did not tell my supervisor.

CONSULTANT PHYSICIAN: I couldn't quit, but I also couldn't do it anymore.

INTERN: I did not call Lifeline. I did not do any of that.

CONSULTANT PHYSICIAN: So—and I was single and having an existential crisis—

Laughs.

And so I, I just—it was funny, because I could go to work every day and I could function normally and look fine and be fine and put up a really good wall.

INTERN: I did not tell my psychologist.

CONSULTANT PHYSICIAN: But then I'd get home and I couldn't even pay my bills, I couldn't shop, I couldn't buy food, I couldn't cook.

INTERN: Because I could be reported and I would lose my job for having those thoughts.

CONSULTANT PHYSICIAN: Just because I couldn't—I was paralysed to do anything except get up, go to work, work hard, come home.

INTERN: Also the worry that I could be put away somewhere and then lose my job.

CONSULTANT PHYSICIAN: I don't know how that happened.

INTERN: So it does stop people from seeking help.

CONSULTANT PHYSICIAN: I wasn't worried about getting reported.

INTERN: I would appreciate it if you would obviously anonymise that.

CONSULTANT PHYSICIAN: That wasn't the barrier to care for me, the barrier to care for me was that I didn't think that they could help me.

INTERN: I mean, you can say it, but just not relate it to me in any way.

CONSULTANT PHYSICIAN: I didn't think that they could help me. What could they do to change my circumstance? They couldn't get me out of this hole that I'm in, they couldn't stop the freight train that I was on. No-one could change my circumstance, so there wasn't any point in asking for help. It wasn't until two and a half years later when I actually got help that I realised had I had help three years earlier this could've all been avoided.

Beat.

I didn't understand that help would work.

Pause.

FORMER SURGEON: People go, 'You're so close. How did you not finish it?' The response I come back with is, 'I would have jumped off a cliff'. For me, that was a mental health risk. That was suicide to finish that for the sake of finishing it. If someone was stuck in an abusive relationship, would you say to them, 'But you're married with kids, make it work. I know he bashes the crap out of you every day but make it work.' No-one would say that. They'd say, 'Leave the bastard'. Why are we not the same in medicine? Because you are going against this system that's not there to support you. So for me that was life and death. It was mental health life and death. It was physical health life and death; I developed a pretty serious medical condition as a result of the stress and pressure that was on my body. I just couldn't justify killing myself at the age of forty-five with a mental health problem—well, if I hadn't have jumped off the cliff that was. I just went, 'You know what?'—excuse my French—'Fuck you and everything that you stand for. I've got a life to live. I don't care if I have to clean toilets for the rest of my life, I'm not putting up with this.'

Beat.

INTERVIEWER: You're not cleaning toilets— /
FORMER SURGEON: No. /
INTERVIEWER: You are—you have rebuilt—you've— /
FORMER SURGEON: My life, yeah.

A long pause.

INTERVIEWER: I'm sure there's good stories as well.
REGISTRAR 2: I was going to say, we sound like—I think we should talk about some good things. I think it would be nice to talk about— /

REGISTRAR 1: About medicine?

REGISTRAR 2: I think I've enjoyed a lot of things in medicine. I think—I enjoy going to work. Like today I had a good day at work. I guess today I felt like I was applying what I had learned to help people and I was learning as well at the same time. Consultants were teaching me, I was teaching junior staff. It was a reasonable day. I've had some hard days as well, but I think an ideal day is—I feel—I've always looked forward to work—I'm enjoying what I'm doing now. Yeah, I think there's a—you know it when you've done something worthwhile.

Beat.

SENIOR NURSE: I can't tell you how—seriously, I can't ever think of the job that would give you the feeling of satisfaction that you get when it goes right, when you feel like you're doing the best job you could possibly do, when you—I can't tell you how good that is. Which sounds a bit over the top, but it's true.

I can—seriously, you can go on a shift and not be feeling one hundred per cent, like a bit of a meh day, something going on at home, you're just feeling a bit of a, like, and you can finish that shift in a great mood. In the best mood because you know that you've gone a good job and you know that people appreciate what you've done for them that day, and you've worked with a great bunch of colleagues.

Nurses have got the best sense of humour. We talk about the maddest things over lunchtime and we always laugh because life can be pretty grim when you work in a hospital. It is a fantastic career and I've loved every minute of it.

Beat.

Even the bad things.

Pause.

INTERN: I do have a couple of examples of really great times that I've had. So I remember as a medical student I did—we had a term in obstetrics and gynaecology and I did a week of nights on the maternity ward. There was this one night, like it was the best week I've ever had in medicine. It was so much fun. There was this one night that was just insane because the midwives were all saying, 'It's a full moon, it means things are going to be crazy'.

I'm not superstitious at all, so I was kind of going, 'That's nonsense'. You know, full of crap. But …

Laughs.

… it was crazy. It was totally crazy. There were eight births that night which I think was one down from their record of nine births in one night. I caught five of them. We also had this moment where we were rushing this woman on a gurney to have an emergency C-section and kind of running down the corridor. That only happens in the movies but it happened to me which was pretty exciting. But the best part of that night was there was a woman giving birth for the first time and I was there to help catch the baby.

It had been a relatively prolonged birth. So it was about three-thirty in the morning at this point. When the baby came out, the umbilical cord was quite short. So she couldn't see the baby. So the doctors cut the cord and then I took the baby to the crib to check them out, make sure everything was going okay, have a listen to the chest, all the things you have to do. Then I swaddled the baby and took the baby to their mother and I had this kind of almost existential moment as I was walking with this child to their parents, where I realised this is the first time they're going to see their child. I'm the person handing their first child to them.

That was really—I really treasure that moment because I just realise that this is so—I get to be part of this person's life in that way. It was so beautiful. It was just so lovely. So I really treasure that moment. Yeah.

Pause.

INTERVIEWER: [to CONSULTANT PHYSICIAN] What about a moment that you're most, most proud of? A moment you're really proud of, where you thought, 'I've done good today'.

CONSULTANT PHYSICIAN: The one that springs to mind—it sounds terrible—helping people die. So I had a patient who—I was a junior registrar, I was on a respiratory term and she had end-stage lung disease from smoking and she was pretty end-stage. One day I came in and she was really sick and I said, 'You're going to have to put the pressure mask on to help you breathe', and she said, 'I can't, I can't have that pressure mask anymore'. I said, 'You need it', and she said, 'I can't, I can't do it, I can't do it'. Then she started gasping for breath. I said, 'You need to, you need to, you need to', and she said, 'No, enough's enough'. I said, 'Okay', and she said, 'Now what?' I said, 'Well, now it's you and me'. 'We can do this,' she said—and then she started gasping and gasping and gasping. I was a junior registrar and I didn't really have the authority to make that call, I guess. But there wasn't—you kind of have to sometimes. I said to the nurse, 'Go and get me ten milligrams of morphine'. The nurse said, 'What?' I said, 'Yep, and ten milligrams of Midazolam, now'. She went and she got it and I rang the consultant and I said, 'She's dying. She doesn't want the mask, she says she's had enough, she's dying.' He said, 'Okay, morphine and Midazolam'. I said, 'Yep, ready to go', and he said, 'Okay'.

   Beat.

So I had the permission of the consultant, the permission of the patient and then there's that double entendre. You can't give the morphine to kill the person, but to relieve the suffering, you're okay. So we stood there and we gave her teensy-weensy little bits of morphine until the suffering stopped. The reason I'm so proud of that is because I was staring into the face of a human who had sheer terror through her eyes and her soul and there was pain and there was terror like you'll never ever, like I will never see again, I don't think.

   Beat.

I stood there and I said, 'It's okay', and I held her hand and I gave her the morphine slowly, slowly, slowly until she was gone.

INTERVIEWER: That's beautiful. I mean, that's what we value, as outsiders. We—you're there when we're born, there when we die, you and the nurses. /

CONSULTANT PHYSICIAN: Yeah, yeah.

INTERVIEWER: It is a great consolation and it's kind of a measure of what makes us human. When my mum died recently—Mum was ninety-three, She'd been a widow for many, many, many years and so forth. But anyway, she'd made it very clear to everyone that no heroics, she had an advanced care directive, all that sort of thing. I used to spend some time with Mum and so, yeah, so something was not right. She was throwing up and vomiting and she was complaining of gut pain and so on and so forth.

Beat.

Off we went to the hospital and it was fantastic. They did some scans and got a result pretty quickly and she had an ischaemic gut and so it was very clear-cut, she's not going to survive that. I was able to get up really close to my mum to say, 'Look, Mum, this is the situation, are you feeling okay with this?' She said, 'Yes, yes, yes, let's just move it along, we're good'. Every single health professional I came into contact with for the—it took my mum forty-eight hours to actually die, every—every one was professional, caring, kind.

CONSULTANT PHYSICIAN: That's good.

INTERVIEWER: It'll make a difference to me for the rest of my life, and it makes a difference to my kids who came in. My kids held my mum's hand and they could see that Nanna wasn't sad, and Nanna was feeling— /

CONSULTANT PHYSICIAN: Your mum's story's going to make me cry. /

INTERVIEWER: And it's the best, and at the very end I was there with my sister and it was very late. Mum, you know, she had that breath. It wasn't a death rattle or anything like that, it was just a— /

CONSULTANT PHYSICIAN: Agonal breathing.

INTERVIEWER: Yeah, it was just kind of a—it was like a, it was very regular, it was like, 'Ho-aaa'.

CONSULTANT PHYSICIAN: Yeah, yep.

INTERVIEWER: 'Ho-aaa', sort of thing, and you just thought, 'Okay, she's just—' It's like a finite number, I don't know what the number is, but she's got to breathe a certain number of breaths and— /

CONSULTANT PHYSICIAN: That's right, yeah. /

INTERVIEWER: —then she'll get to the last one and that's when she wants to go. It's like it's late, it's like two o'clock in the morning or something, and I said to my sister, 'Oh, do you think she's going to make it until morning?' My sister said, 'I don't know, maybe'. Everyone had been predicting she would be dead quite some time before. I said, 'Well look, let's just—' I moved the bed a little bit and I made room for two little mattresses next to the bed for—that the nurses supplied, and my sister and me would lay down and it was just like we were camping.

CONSULTANT PHYSICIAN: Nice.

INTERVIEWER: Like kids on a camping trip and we barely put our heads down and then the next thing I'm aware of this little light, a night light on in the room and it's one of the nurses had come to give her her four-hourly pain relief. Just as my sister and I look up the nurse kind of looks at us and so we realised Mum had just breathed her last breath, amazing. Then we said to the nurses, 'Oh, so—' And we weren't sobbing or anything, it was just like, 'Mum, that's incredible that you've done that, you've done that so beautifully, you waited'. /

CONSULTANT PHYSICIAN: She knew. /

INTERVIEWER: She knew, and we said to the nurses, 'So, what happens now? I guess, what, do you have to wash the body?' They said, 'Yes, yes, we'll wash your mother before she goes down to the morgue', and we said, 'Oh, can we help?' Because both my sister and I had often helped Mum showering and stuff, we knew that Mum wouldn't be— /

CONSULTANT PHYSICIAN: Yeah, offended. /

INTERVIEWER: —bothered or offended. The nurses just came, just brought us a basin and said, 'You do it, do you need any help?' We did it together. The nurses just said, 'You can do it if you're fine', and my sister said, 'Oh, is it okay if I—I've brought some of Mum's bath oil'. It was like, she was smelling so beautiful. /

CONSULTANT PHYSICIAN: That's so nice.

INTERVIEWER: We washed her body and, but everyone in the hospital facilitated that.

CONSULTANT PHYSICIAN: That's beautiful.

INTERVIEWER: So, you know, I thought I should share because you shared so much.

CONSULTANT PHYSICIAN: Thank you.

INTERVIEWER: I think we're done here, I'll just, I'll …

THE END

SEYMOUR CENTRE & THE
BIG ANXIETY — FESTIVAL OF
ARTS + SCIENCE + PEOPLE
PRESENT

GRACE UNDER PRESSURE

by David Williams & Paul Dwyer
in collaboration with the Sydney Arts & Health Collective

Seymour Centre
25 – 28 OCT

Performers RENEE LIM, ROSE MAHER, SAL SHARAH
& WENDY STREHLOW
Director DAVID WILLIAMS
Dramaturg PAUL DWYER
Lighting Designer RICHARD MANNER
Sound Designer GAIL PRIEST
Set & Costume Designer ISABEL HUDSON
Production Manager EMMA BEDFORD
Stage Manager PATRICK HOWARD
Producer DAVID WILLIAMS (for Seymour Centre)

*Grace Under Pressure has been co-commissioned by Seymour Centre and The Big Anxiety,
and developed with the support of the Department of Performance Studies, University
of Sydney. The Big Anxiety has been assisted by the Australian government through the
Department of Communication and the Arts' Catalyst—Australian Arts and Culture Fund.*

FOREWORD

How did we start a project to counteract bullying in healthcare workplaces and end up with a piece of theatre? I blame the Internet and Augusto Boal.

Medical education can be a very dry place … a litany of scientific facts and figures that need to be learned by rote and regurgitated on demand. But apart from the so-called 'hard sciences' of physiology, anatomy and clinical studies, there is also the need to acquire knowledge that is all too often given the somewhat derogatory title of 'soft science'. And so I find myself trying to enthuse cohort after cohort of eager young clinicians on the necessity of topics like communication, ethics, cultural diversity and the negative impact of minority stress on health outcomes.

What now seems like an age ago in early 2015, I started writing about my distress at the continuing deaths of young doctors and medical students who succumbed to the stresses of the profession. But that journey for me had really started on the first day of medical school, as it has done for so many other doctors before and since.

"No doctor ever forgets the excruciating fear of that first day, first week, on the job. Tragically, for some, the fear doesn't go away. In the nearly forty years since I started medical school, I have known of a number of suicides of colleagues and friends. [These] are simply the tip of an iceberg buoyed by the many that tried and failed, thought about it and changed their minds, numbed their pain with drugs and alcohol, or walked away from the profession completely in order to keep body and soul together. [...] Simply asking the questions, "So why didn't they get help?" or "why wasn't help provided?" ignores the very significant determinants of psychological distress in the medical community and the barriers to accessing care."

Kimberley Ivory, 'A call for medicine to stop devouring its young', https://blogs.crikey.com.au/croakey/2015/02/06/a-call-for-medicine-to-stop-devouring-its-young/

We speak colloquially of health as the "caring" professions, yet there is ample evidence of the damage that doctors and nurses do to one another. Bullying, harassment and "teaching by humiliation" (Scott, Caldwell et al. 2015) are a common experience in hospitals, particularly for students and junior staff. Rates of clinical depression and anxiety, suicidal ideation and suicidal behaviours among this population are twice the national average. (BeyondBlue 2013)

Looking at that data from Beyond Blue, it quickly became clear that the same identities that commonly experience marginalization in the wider community also suffer in medicine: women and the young, Indigenous students or those from a different ethnicity, and students who have a mental health condition. These same groups are also the ones most likely to report experiences of bullying and harassment in medicine. (Fnais, Soobiah et al. 2014) The story is repeated across disciplines. Dentists, nurses, pharmacist and physiotherapists also report similar grievances from similar demographics, suggesting that complex cultural factors contribute to how abuse is perpetuated within the healthcare workplace. (Rees, Monrouxe et al. 2015)

In reality, this should not be surprising. On one level, it merely indicates that health workers are human. Health is not unique. Discrimination, bullying and harassment sadly occur in every workplace. When we started this project we had vets and lawyers keen to sign on. The theory behind why marginalized people have poorer mental health outcomes is that social exclusion – lack of social connectedness – the product of stigma and discrimination, is a negative social determinant of health that leads to mental distress, substance abuse, reduced access to health care and poorer health outcomes.

So the question was not really 'how' this had become a feature of healthcare culture, but rather, 'what' could be done about it? One of the advantages of working in a major university is the access it provides to experts in just about anything you can imagine. In earlier attempts to find creative ways to get my students to appreciate the role of diversity and minority stress on health, I had searched the university intranet for someone with an interest in using applied theatre in medical education. I struck gold. I found Dr Paul Dwyer, then chair of the department of Performance Studies. Paul had written his PhD on Augusto Boal and the Theatre of the Oppressed and is an expert in reparative theatre. To top it off he is almost the sole non-health professional in his entire extended family. For a lay person, he has a unique understanding of medical culture and what it means to be a doctor.

It seemed like a kind of victim blaming to try to tackle the culture of bullying and harassment in healthcare, simply by teaching our students to be more resilient, as many earlier programs had attempted. Instead, we sought an approach that would encourage and reinforce positive behaviours from all involved and ultimately result in generational change. Having successfully collaborated with Paul in 2012 (Ivory, Dwyer et al. 2016) and having witnessed the impact of forum theatre on medical student's ability to better hear and understand the patient's story, it seemed only logical to call on him and Augusto again to see what theatre could offer those distressed and wounded by a brutal system.

The result was the pilot series of interactive theatre skills workshops given the working title, *Grace under Pressure*, and the birth of the Sydney Arts and Health Collective (SAHC) with founding members from different schools across Sydney University: Dr Claire Hooker and Associate Professor Paul MacNeill (Sydney Health Ethics), Dr Jo River (Nursing), Dr Karen Scott (Medical Education), Dr Paul Dwyer (Performance Studies), Associate Professor Louise Nash (Brain and Mind Centre) and Dr Kimberley Ivory (Sydney Public Health). The workshops' theatre techniques included Boal's image theatre exercises in which theatrical debate allows participants to

observe, comment on and intervene in scenarios that dramatize oppressive social situations, examining the scope for individual or collective action. Boal's intent for his theatre of the oppressed was to free the audience from the traditional constraints or oppression of the theatre itself and turn them into *spect-actors*, employing the pedagogical theories of Paulo Freire that see education as a means of consciously shaping the person and the society. The initial workshops were trialed on medical students, (Scott, Berlec et al. 2016) then rolled out to hospital doctors and other staff in urban and rural settings, eventually being taken up interstate and showcased at a range of local and international conferences.

Since the first days of this project, we received stories from students, doctors, nurses and their families about terrible experiences in healthcare settings. We felt an over-riding need to do justice to these stories, the trust their authors showed in us and their hopes that things would improve for others. "Verbatim theatre" grew in our thinking as our next step for a catalyst to promote culture change.

A chat with theatre director David Williams and a small grant round allowed us to propose an entirely new project investigating the challenges that clinical students, junior staff face in their training and professional identity formation using verbatim theatre. Further grants came from The Big Anxiety Festival (UNSW), Sydney Public Health, an Education Innovation grant from Sydney University and support from the Seymour Centre.

Verbatim theatre is a research and performance methodology that uses phenomenological, observational and interview data to create a play, often in collaboration with its research subjects. The performance then prompts discussion and engagement with its various audiences. Building on the stories we already had, we interviewed almost 30 people working across the breadth of health care: eg students, junior and senior doctors, junior and senior nurses, paramedic and administration in order to explore in depth questions about how healthcare workers experience, survive, challenge, disrupt, build resilience to and survive the bullying, harassment and discrimination that our earlier research identified as rife within the hierarchical work cultures of health.

David and Paul wrestled those transcribed interviews into a very powerful, engaging piece of theatre about health workplace training and culture. They spent hours pouring over press clippings, articles and blogs about the experiences of both nurses and doctors to also discover the internecine violence in healthcare extended to violence from patients and patients' families towards nurses and doctors. Who cares for the carers?

The resulting performance is also part of a larger, continuing research project further exploring positive ways to counter many of the negative impacts on the health and well-being of trainees. Transforming interview data into a theatre piece adds a new level of analysis, one that explores how people *enact* their roles and *perform* their identities, modulating performance and presentation to those they 'play' to and against. By re-presenting and exploring the dimensions of the data, the play and its performance, too, constitute new modes of analysis.

Our interviewees shared accounts of behaviours and situations that were experienced as disturbing, disquieting, unprofessional, upsetting, abusive and the like. Every interviewee had their share of "war stories" to tell, so we tried to select those we hoped would connect most immediately with a general public audience and make clear the broader systemic issues highlighted by these individual stories. And, yes, we also included some of the many expressions of joy and humour that percolated through the interviews. As much as the interviews highlighted problems in the culture of health workplaces, they also revealed, over and over again, the satisfaction that health workers find when they are supported to provide quality care for their patients — and for their peers.

Try as we might to come up with a new, dynamic title for this unique work, *Grace Under Pressure* stuck, and the show premiered at the Seymour Centre in Sydney as part of the Big Anxiety Festival in October 2017. But the title was fitting because we not only came away from these interviews with a sense of urgency about the need for culture reform, but also a sense of wonder for the skills and, yes, grace that health workers bring to their job. We think that is what our audiences experienced too. *Grace Under Pressure* helped to open a critical space for conversation about these often-taboo issues, and is an important public intervention into medical culture, as well as a compelling, confronting, hopeful and deeply moving work of theatre.

Kimberley Ivory
Ulaanbaatar, Mongolia

GRACE UNDER PRESSURE:
THE POWER OF CREATIVE ARTS IN HEALTH

The creative arts are beginning to change, not just the face, but the soul of health care. Improving wellbeing through creativity is not new, but it has newly become prominent. Australians are beginning to see the transformations that taking dancing and community art-making into nursing homes, music into rehabilitation centres, drumming into schools, and experimental performance into the public arena can bring.

It's not hard to see why. Artwork of all genres give us so much more insight into the multiple, fragile and frangible dimensions of people's experience; and these understandings generate processes of compassion and empathy. For this reason, visual and expressive works produced by patients have long been valued as a way for doctors to see beyond the breakdown of body parts, and get a sense of the patient's experience of illness.

In Grace Under Pressure, the tables are turned. The public is, for once, invited to understand the experiences of doctors and nurses. And this takes some courage. Culturally, we do not want nurses and doctors to be imperfect. Patients, suddenly vulnerable and frightened, carers bewildered and angered by opaque health care systems, want their clinicians to be invincible. As the play reveals, the culture of medicine (not always nursing) can enforce standards of perfection with harsh and punitive norms and practices. Grace Under Pressure asks the public to 'hold space' for nurses and doctors and look with empathy at their suffering and stumbling.

Art makes ethical demands of its audiences – and does not foreclose their responses, an absence of didacticism that gives moral issues more poignancy. Grace Under Pressure does not merely invite sympathy over the demands that clinical training places on student doctors or the humiliations that result from loud and public criticism by senior clinicians. It begs uncomfortable questions about what price the public is happy to pay for pressures placed on health care systems that are intended to care for them. It asks us to consider what emotional generosity the act – and we mean act – of caring demands, and what caring for our carers might require. It presses upon us the questions, where is the pressure in this system? And where and how is there grace – by which we mean graciousness, compassion, the enacting of care – that is the core of health care?

Verbatim theatre quite explicitly belongs to theatre traditions that have the ethics of witnessing and the aim of engendering social change at their core. Grace Under Pressure was conceived in part as a means of starting public conversations about our precious, fragile, costly, and too often taken-for-granted health system. Public services are as critical to civil society, just as conversations are critical to democratic ones. Grace Under Pressure is inflected with hope and disappointment and pain, just as so many illness journeys also are. But those are reasons to change and treat and heal, and for communal discussions about the kinds of health care systems and cultures that we want, to take place for the sake of us all.

Claire Hooker
Sydney Arts and Health Collective

BIOGRAPHIES

DAVID WILLIAMS Co-Writer/Director/Producer

David is a leading Australian theatre artist whose productions open spaces for public conversation about political and social issues. He was the Curator of ATF 2015: MAKING IT, and has worked for 20 years as a director, writer, producer, dramaturg, and performer with companies across Australia. David was the founder and artistic leader of the performance group version 1.0, and co-created and produced all of the company's work from 1998-2012. He holds a PhD from UNSW, and is currently the Producer/Programmer at the Seymour Centre.

Under the banner DW Projects, David Williams creates theatre works of social relevance, aesthetic rigour and emotional impact from research, interviews, transcripts and public documents. Current and upcoming DW Projects include: *Quiet Faith* (national tour April-July 2018), *Smurf In Wanderland* (National Theatre of Parramatta & Griffin Theatre Company) and *Grace Under Pressure* (Seymour Centre & The Big Anxiety).

PAUL DWYER Co-Writer/ Dramaturg

Paul is a Senior Lecturer in the Department of Theatre and Performance Studies at the University of Sydney. He has published widely on applied theatre, in particular the work of Augusto Boal, and is currently completing a monograph on discourse and performance in restorative justice conferencing. Paul is also a performance maker with extensive professional experience in documentary theatre, including THE BOUGAINVILLE PHOTOPLAY PROJECT, which toured throughout Australia and won a Melbourne Green Room Award, and BEAUTIFUL ONE DAY, a collaboration with Ilbijerri Theatre, Belvoir St Theatre, version 1.0 and members of the Aboriginal and Torres Strait Islander communities of Palm Island.

RENEE LIM Performer

Renee Lim is a performer, educator and medical doctor. In addition to her appearances on Australian TV shows likes *Pulse, Ask The Doctors, East West 101* and *Please Like Me*, and theatre works like *His Mothers Voice* and *Coup De'Tat*, Renee works as the Director of Program Development at the Pam McLean Centre (a centre designed to improve communication in the medical sector) as well as the University of Sydney and UNSW. She is also a locum doctor in Emergency and Geriatrics Departments across NSW, and works in Educational technology and research. She is very excited to be a part of such an important project, as she is focused on well-being and mental health in all her work, including the platform, nayinthelife.com, a collaboration with writer, Clare Hennessy

ROSE MAHER Performer

Rose Maher is a graduate of the University of Wollongong with Honours in Creative Arts, Performance (2013). Rose has also trained with the Shakespeare & Company in Lennox, Massachusetts and will return to complete teacher training in January 2018. Currently a teaching artist with the Faculty of the Arts, English and Media at the University of Wollongong, Rose also works as a children's entertainer with the Starlight Children's Foundation. Her theatre credits include *thirty-three*, Cathode Ray Tube 2016; *GodFace*, Matriark Puppet Theatre 2015; *Erase*, Shopfront Theatre, *Electra*, No White Elephant, both 2013; and with the University of Wollongong *Far Away, Loveplay, The Love of a Nightgale, Pre-paradise Sorry Now, As I Lay Dreaming, Attempts on Her Life* and *The Country*. Film credits include *thirty-three* and *Red Slumber* both with Cathode Ray Tube. Rose is a mean recycler, a mother of succulents and member of the MEAA.

SAL SHARAH Performer

Sal was most recently seen in *Where the Streets Had a Name* for Monkey Baa, *The Incredible Here and Now* for National Theatre of Parramatta and *Hakawati* for National Theatre of Parramatta/Sydney Festival. Other theatre credits include *Jump for Jordan* (Griffin); *Miss Julie, The Rise and Fall of Little Voice* (Sydney Theatre Company); *Les Enfants du Paradis* (Belvoir); *Felliniada* (Belvoir/Auto de Fe); *Salome* (Crossroads); *My Son the Lawyer is Drowning* (Ensemble Theatre); *Alex & Eve* (Bulldog Theatre Company); His musical theatre highlights include the original Australian productions of *Grease, Godspell, The Rocky Horror Show* and Reg Livermore's *Ned Kelly* as well as roles in *My Fair Lady, Sunset Boulevard, Guys and Dolls, Great Expectations* and *The Gambler*. Television includes *The Code, Rake, East West 101, All Saints, Wild Side, GP, Heartbreak High* and *Restless Years*. Films include *The River, Alex & Eve, The Boys, Chain Reaction, Hostage* and *The Custodian*.

WENDY STREHLOW Performer

Since graduating from NIDA, Wendy gained the role of 'Sister Judy Loveday' in *A Country Practice*, for which she also won a Logie Award for Best Supporting Actress. Wendy has extensive television credits, including *McLeod's Daughters*, *All Saints*, *Blue Heelers*, *Halifax f.p.*, *The Saddle Club* and *Home and Away*. Her screen credits include *Dalkeith*, *Dead End*, *Act of Necessity* and *Hoodwink*. Her theatre credits include: *Cyrano de Bergerac*, *Love's Labour's Lost*, *The Importance of Being Earnest*, *The Crucible* and *A Midsummer Night's Dream* for Sport for Jove; *Machinal* for Sydney Theatre Company; *Travesties*, *Broken Glass*, *The Norman Conquests* and *Clyborne Park* for the Ensemble Theatre; *Henry IV* and *Taming of the Shrew* for Bell Shakespeare; *Bang for B Sharp*, *Hysteria* for Darlinghurst Theatre Company. Wendy's performance with Tamarama Rock Surfer's *I Want to Sleep With Tom Stoppard* garnered nominations for a Sydney Theatre Award and a Glug Award.

RICHARD MANNER Lighting Designer

Richard is a lighting and AV designer, production manager and IT specialist. He is a past student of the College of Fine Arts, University of NSW (1991), and since then has worked with a range of independent artists and companies. He has held roles at PACT Centre for Emerging Artists, and was Performance Space's Technical Manager from 1999-2011. He is presently the Technical Director at the Department of Theatre and Performance Studies at Sydney University, a position he has held since 2012. At Performance Space, Richard managed the technical aspects over 400 events across visual arts, performance, dance and technology-based practice. He was AV Designer and Operator for version 1.0's national Mobile States tour of *The Bougainville Photoplay Project* which was presented at PICA, Brisbane Powerhouse, and Artshouse in 2010, and was also lighting designer for *The Piper* by My Darling Patricia for Sydney Festival (2014).

GAIL PRIEST Sound Designer

Gail is a Sydney-based artist with a multi-faceted practice in which sound is the key material of communication and investigation. Originally trained in theatre she has worked as a sound designer/composer for performance collaborating with independent directors and choreographers such as Martin del Amo, Jane McKernan, David Williams and Andrea James. She has exhibited her own sound-based installation work nationally and internationally, most recently as part of Experimenta Make Sense, Melbourne and national tour, ISEA2016 Hong Kong, Werkleitz Festival Germany and at UTS Gallery, Sydney in an exhibition she also curated. She has released several albums of exploratory music through her own label Metal Bitch as well as Flaming Pines and Endgame records. She writes extensively about sound and media arts, in particular for RealTime magazine, as well as being the editor of *Experimental Music: audio explorations in Australia* through UNSW Press (2009). She was the 2015/2016 Australia Council Emerging and Experimental Arts Fellow.

ISABEL HUDSON Set & Costume Designer

Isabel is a Sydney-based production designer and graduate of the NIDA design course (2015) and holds a Bachelor of Arts (Screen and Sound) from UNSW (2012). Isabel was awarded the William Fletcher Foundation Tertiary Grant for emerging artists in 2015. Recently, Isabel has designed Set and Costumes for: *One Flew over the Cuckoo's Nest* (Sport for Jove), *I love you now* (Darlinghurst Theatre Company), *The Plant* (Ensemble Theatre Company), *The Merry Widow* (Opera Australia – Assistant Set Designer to Michael Scott Mitchell), *Intersections* (ATYP), *The Shadowbox, Hurt* and *Blackrock* (White Box Productions), *The Block Universe* and *Journeys End* (Cross Pollinate), *The Chamber Pot Opera* (Bontom; Sydney, Adelaide and Edinburgh seasons), *Slut* (Festival Fatale), and worked as an associate on Opera Australia's *My Fair Lady*. In 2015 Isabel designed *A Dream Play* directed by Kim Carpenter, *Top Girls* directed by Susanna Dowling, *Love and Honour* and *Pride and Pity and Compassion and Sacrifice*, directed by Priscilla Jackman.

EMMA BEDFORD Production Manager

Emma Bedford is committed to the diverse, eclectic world of live entertainment. Emma has extensive experience in production management and as a professional audio describer. In recent years Emma has worked for Performance Space, Sydney Festival, version 1.0, WOMADelaide, Vitalstatistix and Adelaide Fringe. She currently works as the Operations Manager for Erth Visual and Physical.

PATRICK HOWARD Stage Manager

Patrick is a freelance theatre artist with a passion for political, devised, queer and documentary theatre. Graduating from AIM Dramatic Arts (formerly AADA) in 2014, he has directed, dramaturged, production and stage managed and sound designed for a number of companies. Notable production credits include *Tribunal* (PYT Fairfield); *Jump First, Ask Later* (PYT Fairfield & Force Majeure); *Business Unfinished* (Tom Christophersen Creates); *Blonde Poison* (Strange Duck Productions, Sydney Opera House, Melbourne Theatre Company); *5 Guys Chillin'*, *That Eye The Sky*, *When the Rain Stops Falling, The School for Scandal* (New Theatre); *Babes in the Woods, Low Level Panic,The Whale, Masterclass 2, Debris* (Red Line Productions) and *Blink* (Stories Like These). His credits as an actor include *Marat/Sade, Mother Clap's Molly House* (New Theatre); *Tender Indifference, Götterdämmerung* (Arrive. Devise. Repeat.) and *Blackrock* (Pilgrim Theatre). Patrick is a founding member of theatre collective Arrive. Devise. Repeat., a play assessor for New Theatre, holds an Honours degree from the Sydney Conservatorium of Music, and is a proud member of MEAA Equity.

www.ingramcontent.com/pod-product-compliance
Lightning Source LLC
Chambersburg PA
CBHW050025090426
42734CB00021B/3419